TRAM TRAVELLERS

ILLUSTRATIONS AND MUSINGS BY SLOBODANKA GRAHAM

TRAM TRAVELLERS

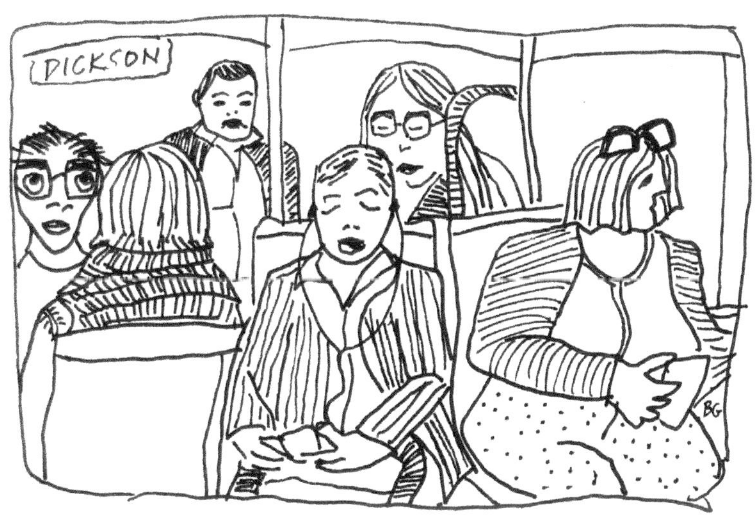

ILLUSTRATIONS AND MUSINGS BY SLOBODANKA GRAHAM

Published by BGPublishers
www.bgpublishers.com.au

On behalf of Antipodigital
www.antipodigital.com.au

The Light Rail facts and figures are for the first stage of the project and will change with any future extensions.

Cover and book design by Elise Knotek, Stripe Design
With illustrations by Slobodanka (Bobby) Graham
Digital editions produced by SunTecIndia
www.suntecindia.com
Printed by Ingram Spark
www.ingramspark.com

First edition 2019

ISBN 978-0-6486686-3-3 (print)
ISBN 978-0-6486686-4-0 (digital)

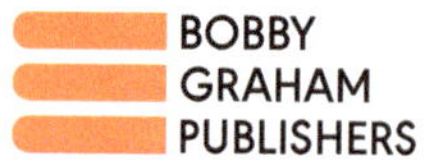

A lovely book with heart warming snapshots taken during a 24mins ride from Gungahlin to Alinga and return. Inspiring sketches well made, displaying the daily operation of Canberra Metro and the people who are riding and working on the railway.

Tilo Franz
General Manager, CMET

This is a brilliant book with lots of appeal visually with Bobby's perceptive, sensitive and attractive drawings of commuters. There is an ethereal quality about the drawings which manage to capture more than the visual image but rather something of the moment in the travellers' lives.

Discover something unique in this beautifully compiled book, something about travelling on a tram...

Franklin Bishop
Author, *The Cartoonist's Bible*

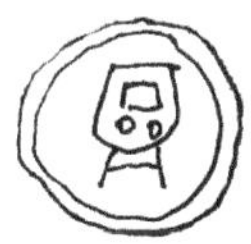

INTRODUCTION

The Canberra Metro Light Rail ran for the first time on 20 April 2019. The development was a long, interesting and controversial project for Canberra. As a Northsider, I watched with anticipation as the works progressed, looking forward to the day when I could catch the tram to work.

There had been many weeks of testing the tram. Empty carriages cruised up and down between Alinga Street and Gunghalin. But on this Saturday, we rode as bona fide commuters for the first time.

Boarding on that first day, I wondered how I should spend my time. I'd already been catching the bus to Civic, which was an hour-long, continuous journey. But the new regime meant I had to catch a bus and a tram to get to the city. How to use my time productively for two short journeys? I took out my sketchbook and pen. → →

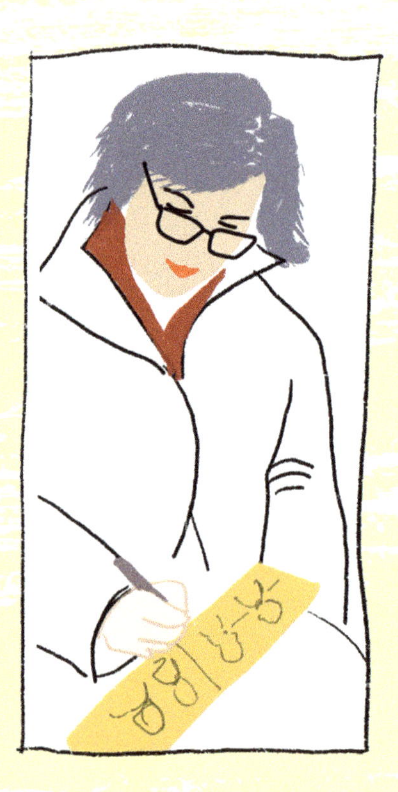

Sketching on a crowded tram is challenging. Often I was hemmed in by people. I could only sketch if I got a seat. It worked best if I sat facing two other people. I was nervous that first morning: what if I drew someone and they hated the experience? I decided my best approach was to sketch quickly. I would complete a drawing in the 20 minutes it took to travel to the city.

I needn't have worried that people would get offended. Most times when I finished a sketch, I'd show it to my subject. And they loved it! I got so much joy out of seeing their smiles and reactions, it kept me motivated to keep on sketching.

As my sketchbook filled up, I decided to produce this little book - to share my sketches, experiences - and the pleasure of travelling by tram with you. This is my homage to the Canberra Metro Light Rail, and the people who ride on it.

BG

Slobodanka Graham

October 2019

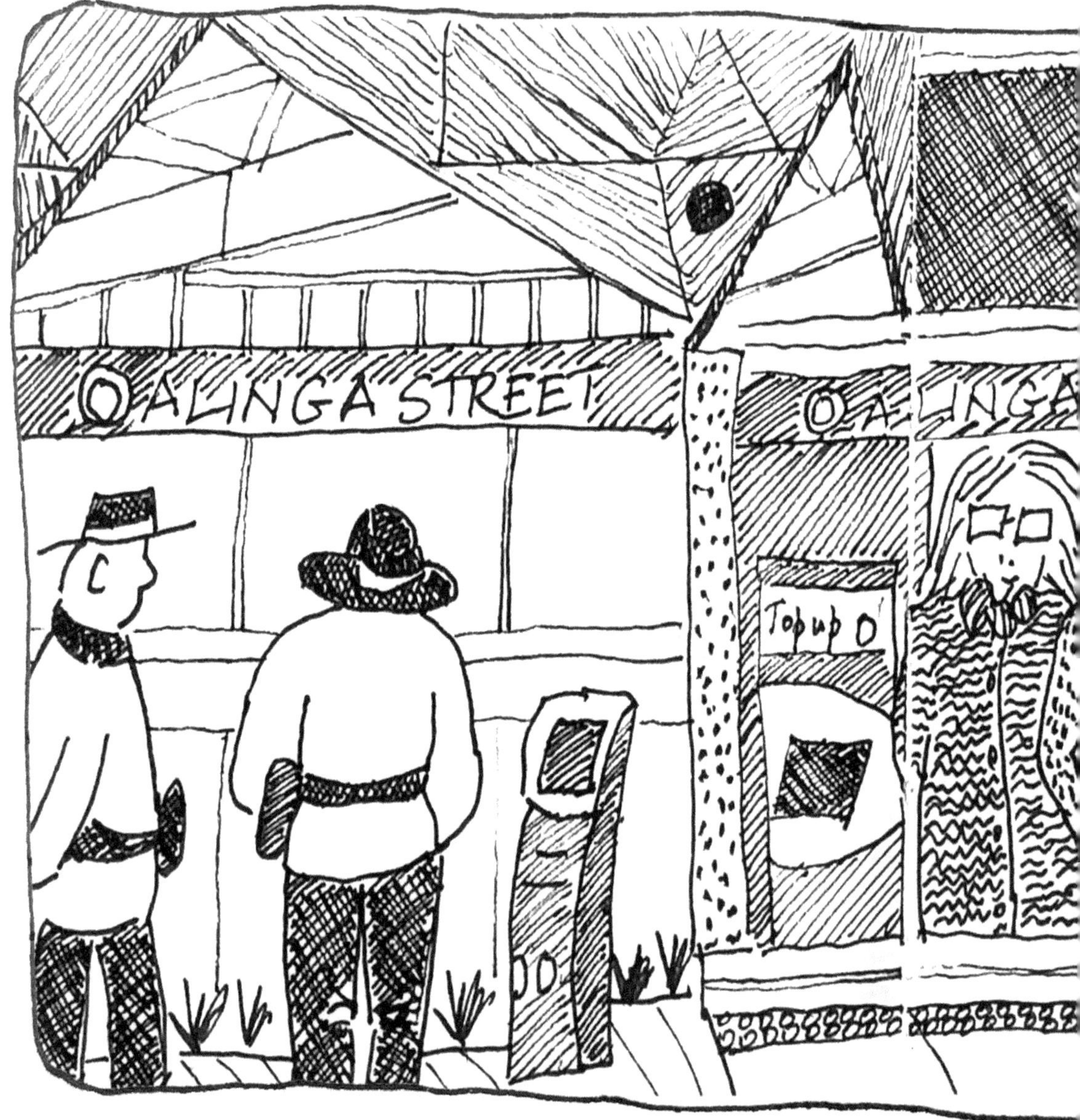
OALINGA STREET
Topup

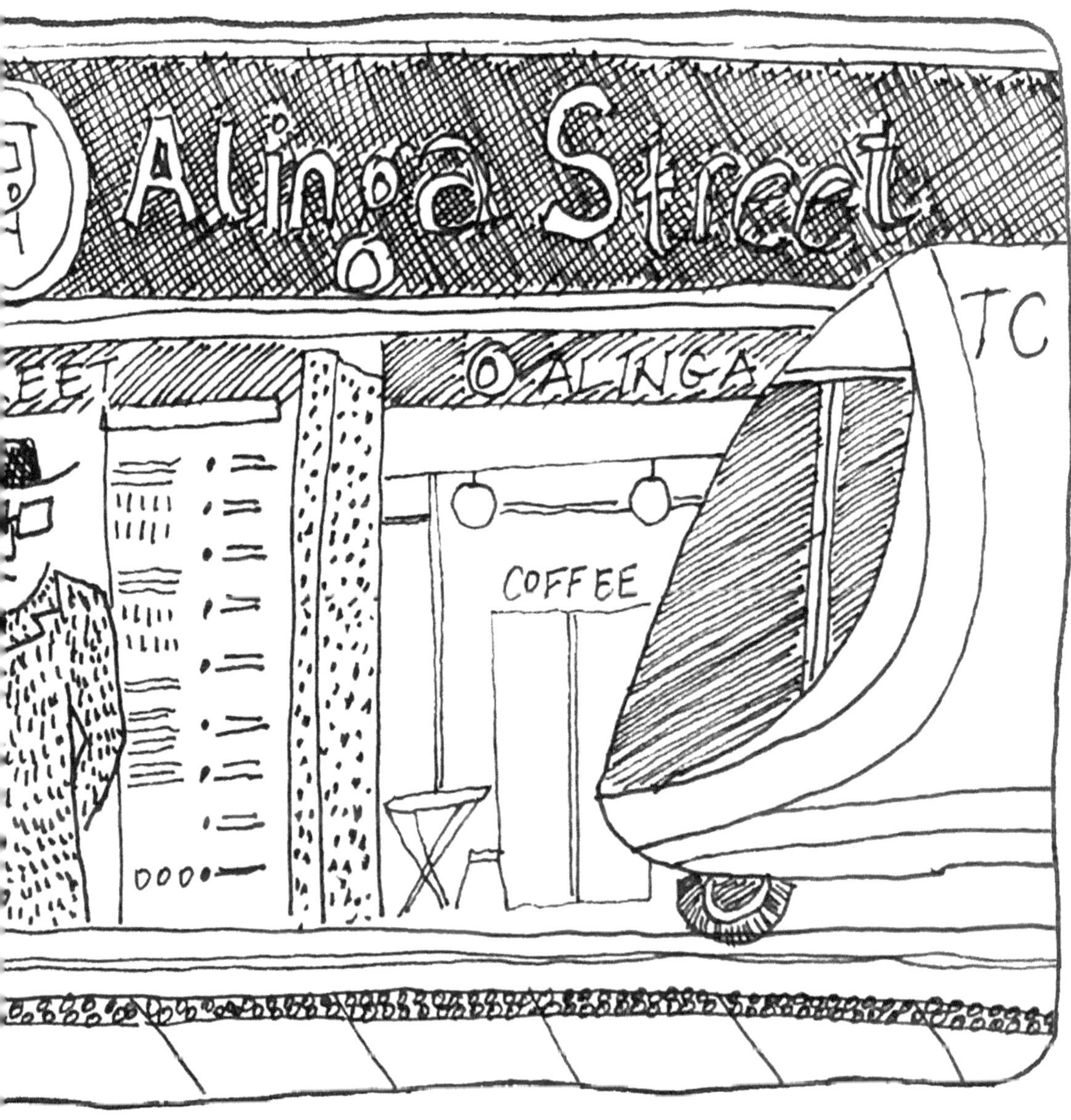
Alinga Street
ALINGA
COFFEE

Alinga Street

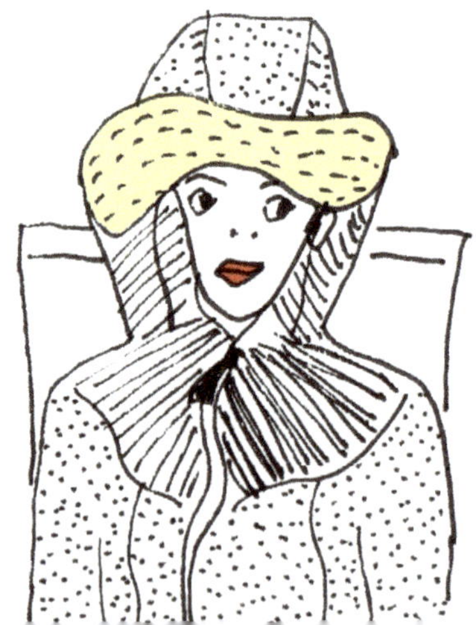

DID YOU KNOW?

It takes 24 minutes to travel from Alinga Street Station to Gunghalin. Or the other way, from Gunghalin to Alinga Street Station.

DID YOU KNOW?

Over weekends and in off-peak times, four Light Rail Vehicles (LRV) operate with a 15-minute headway.

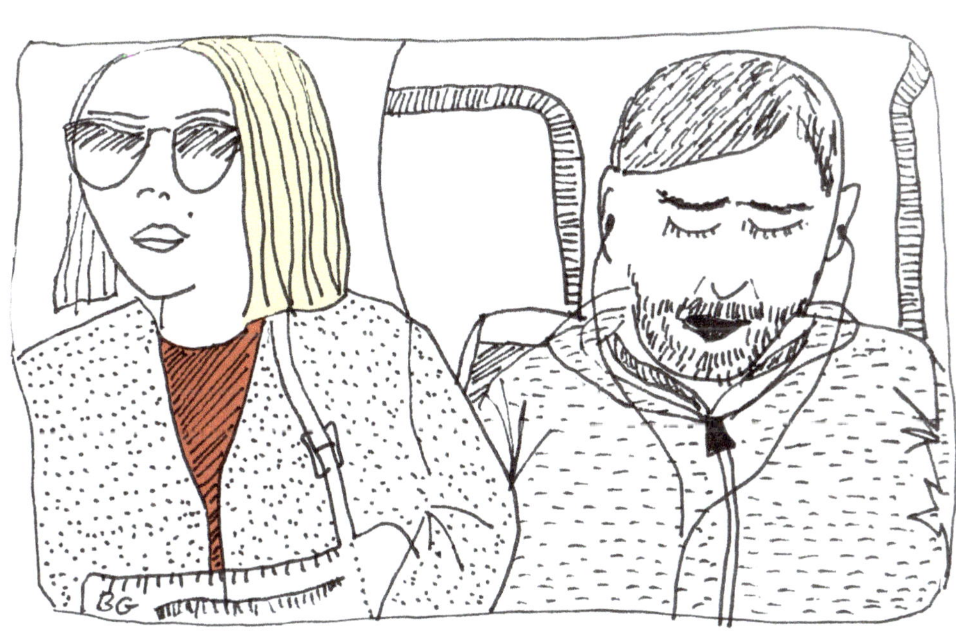
BG

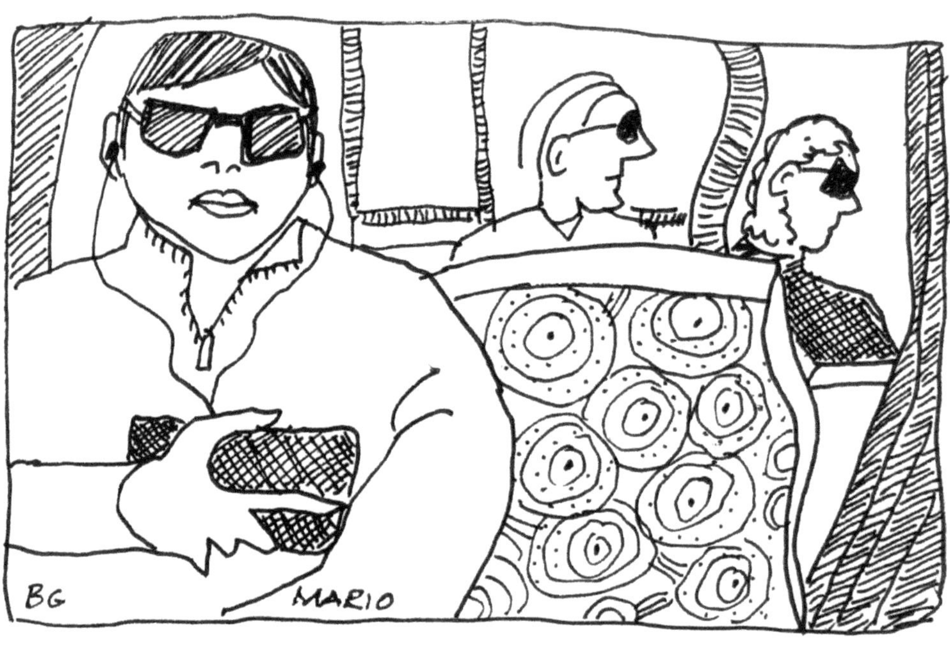
BG
MARIO

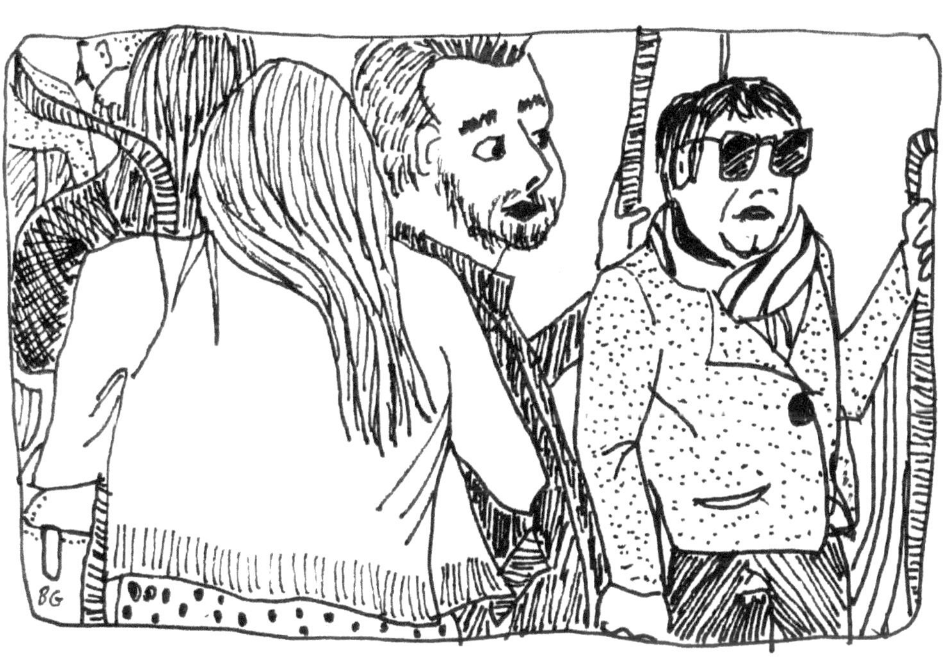
BG

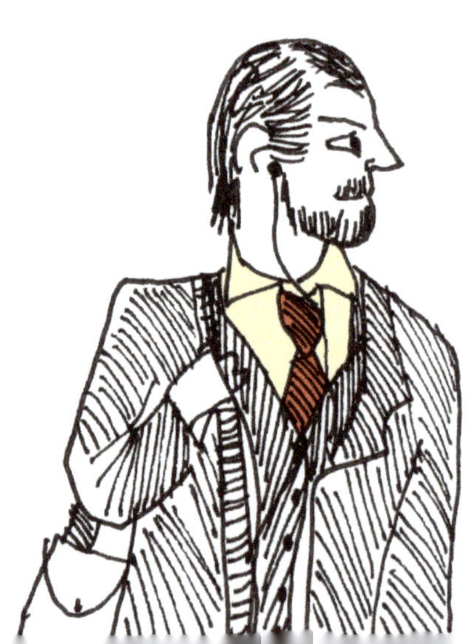

DID YOU KNOW?

There are 14 Light Rail Vehicles in total.

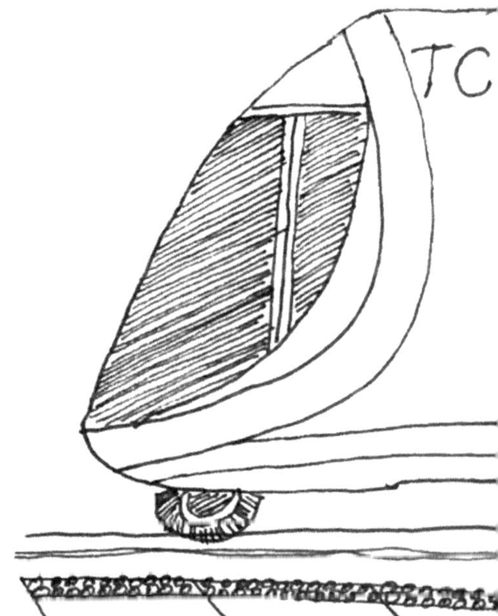

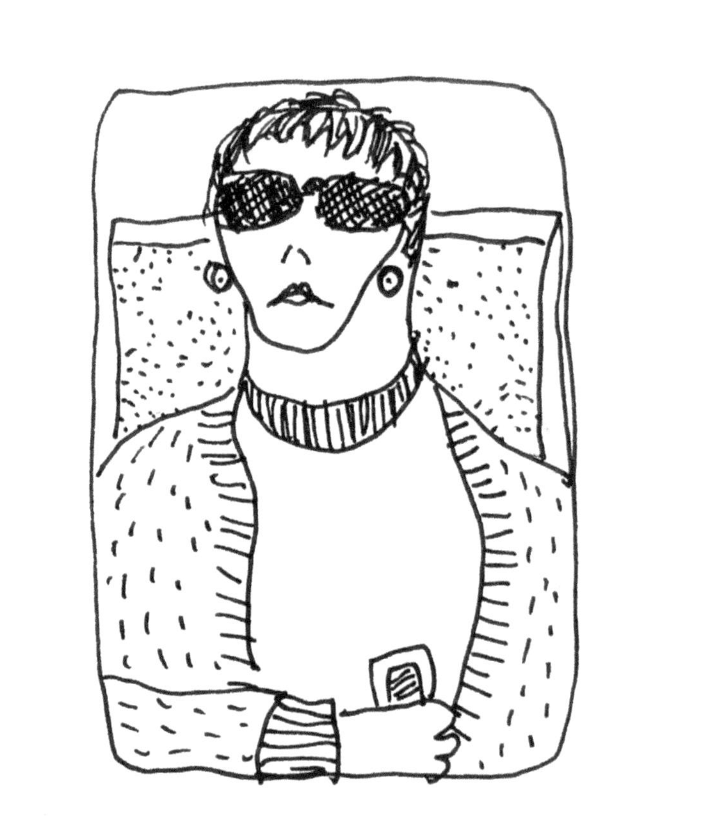

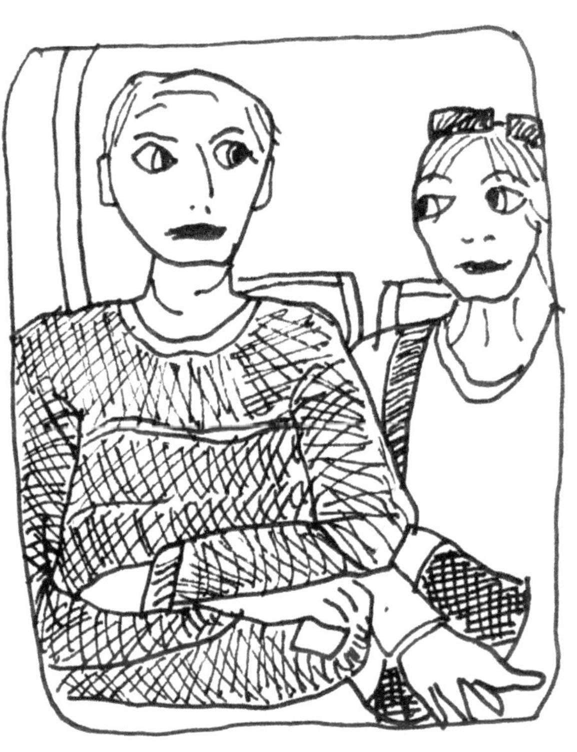

DID YOU KNOW?

The light rail line is 12 kilometres long.

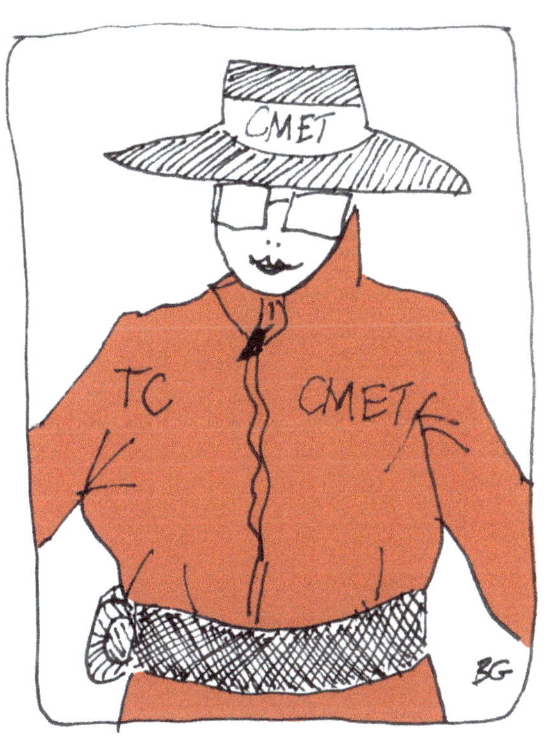
CMET
TC
CMET
BG

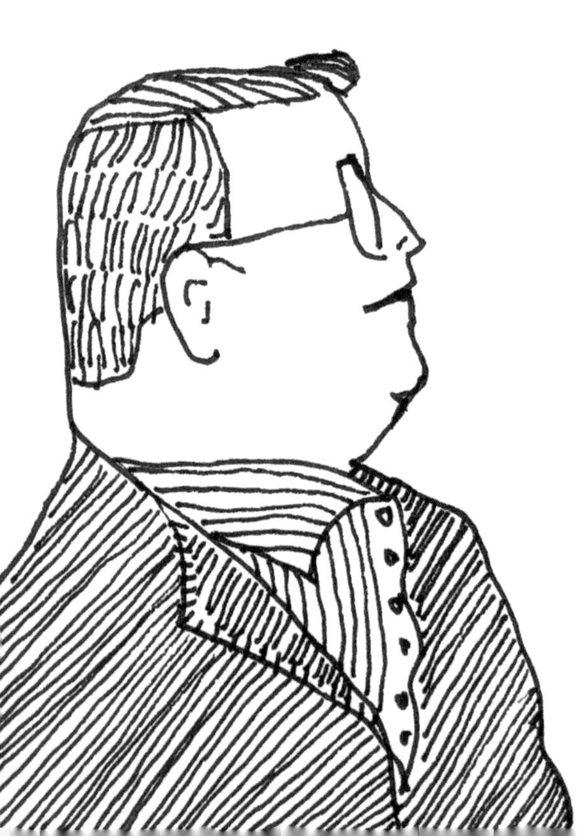

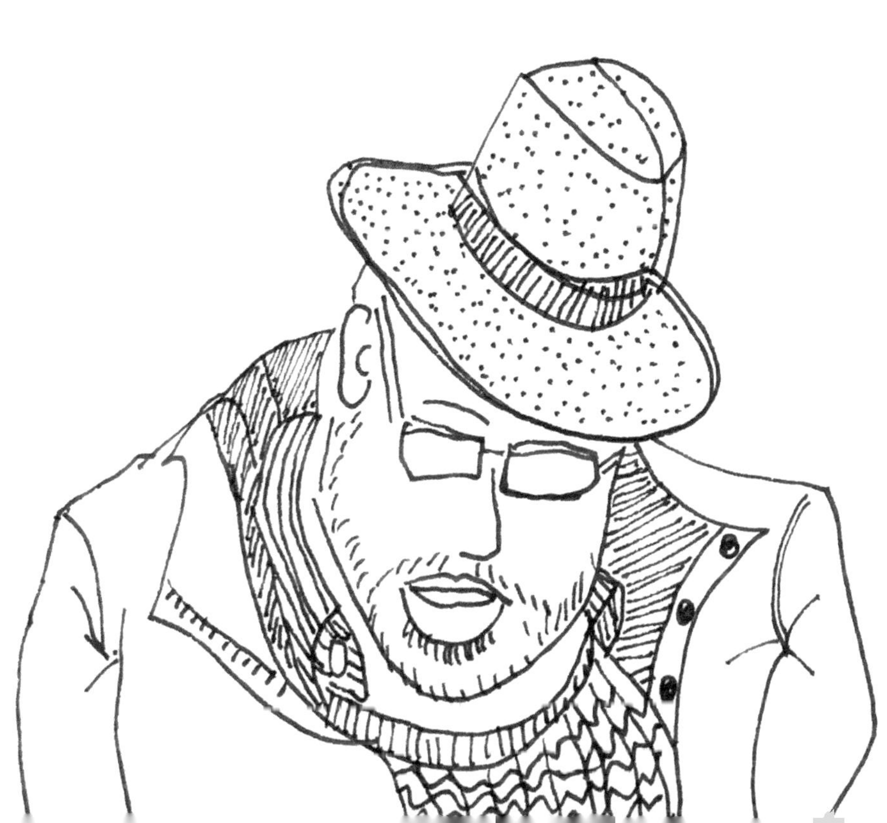

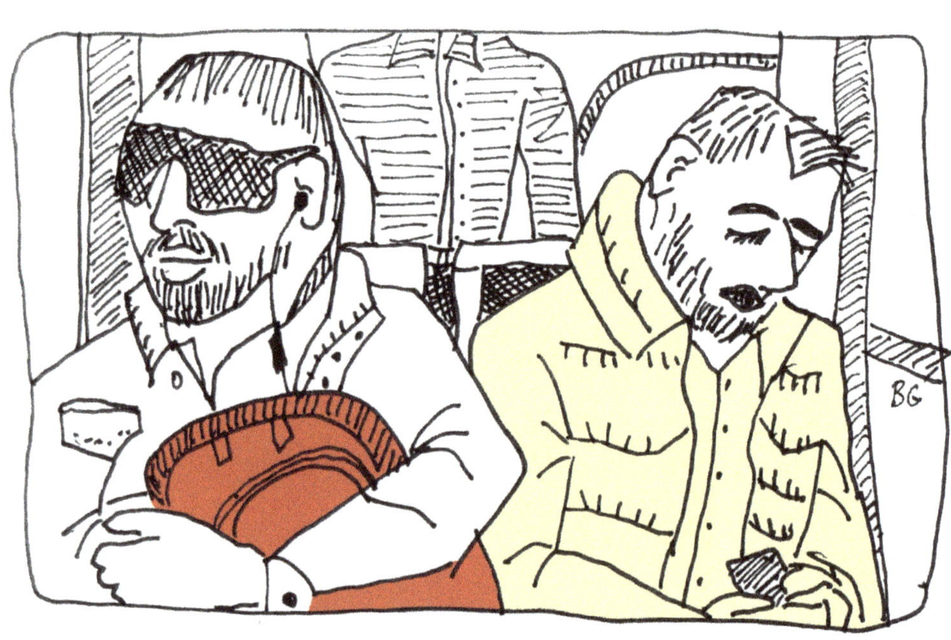
BG

DO YOU KNOW HOW FAST THE LRVs GO?

LRVs travel up to 70 kilometres per hour on parts of the Federal Highway and Flemington Road.

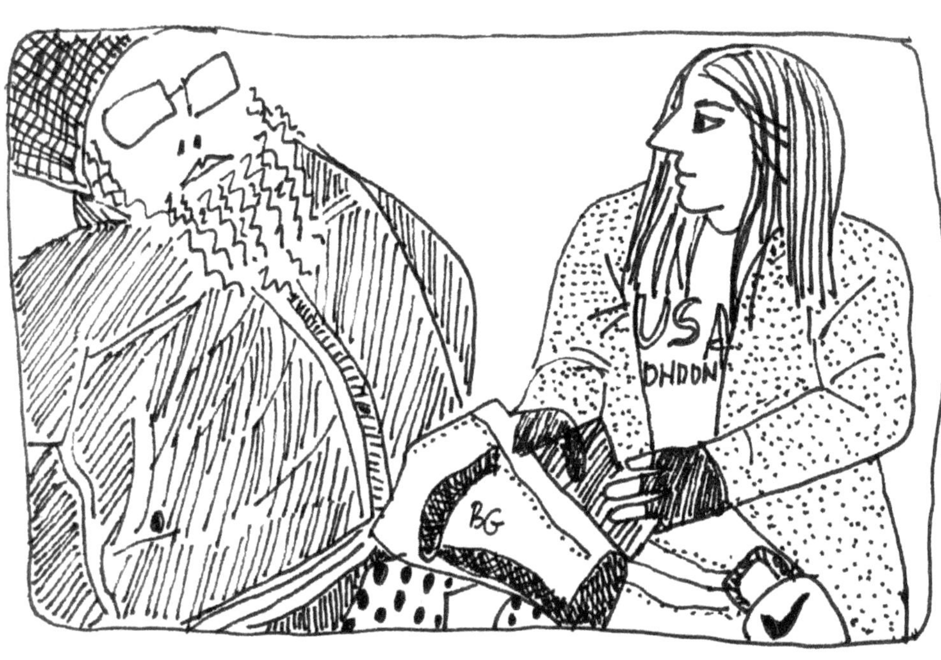
USA
BG

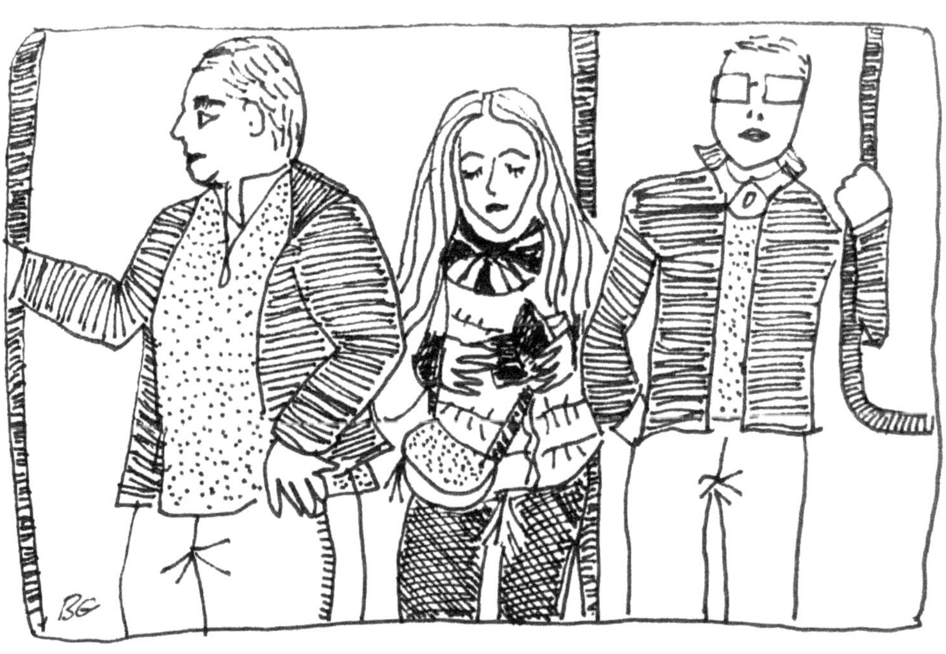
BG

DID YOU KNOW?

Our light rail system has more than one million plants in the corridor.

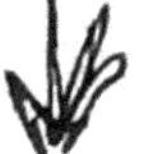
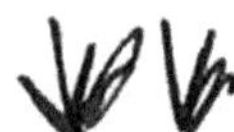
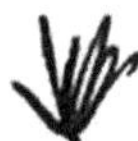
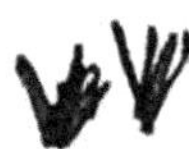

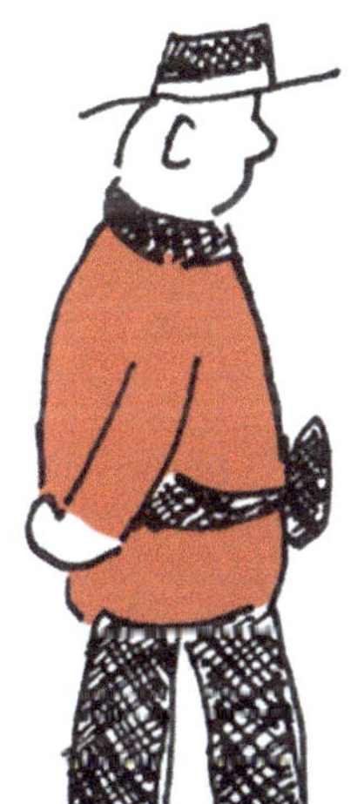
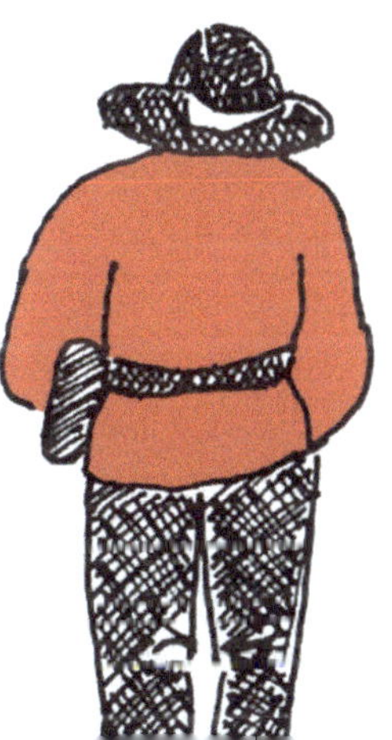

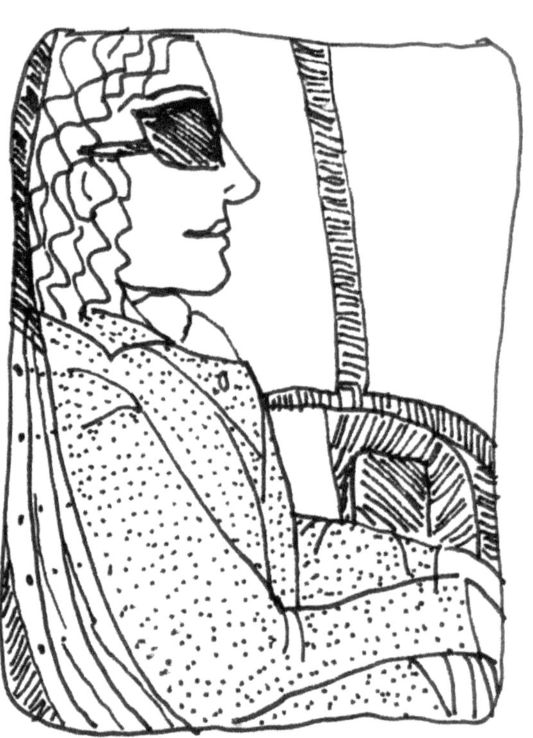

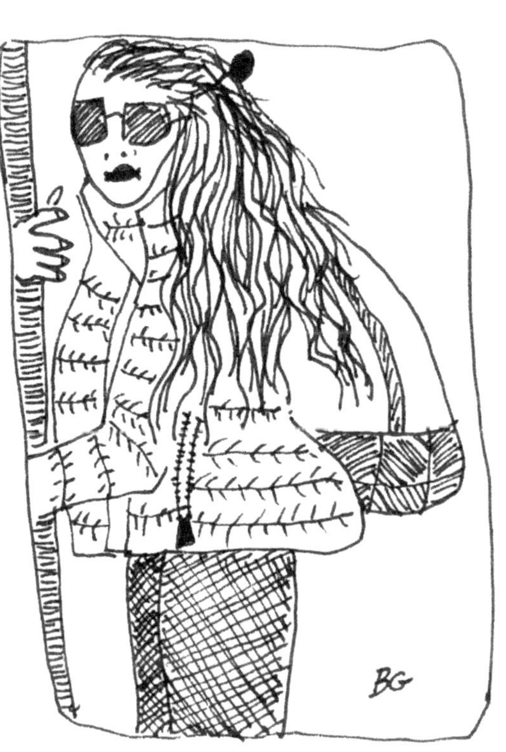
BG

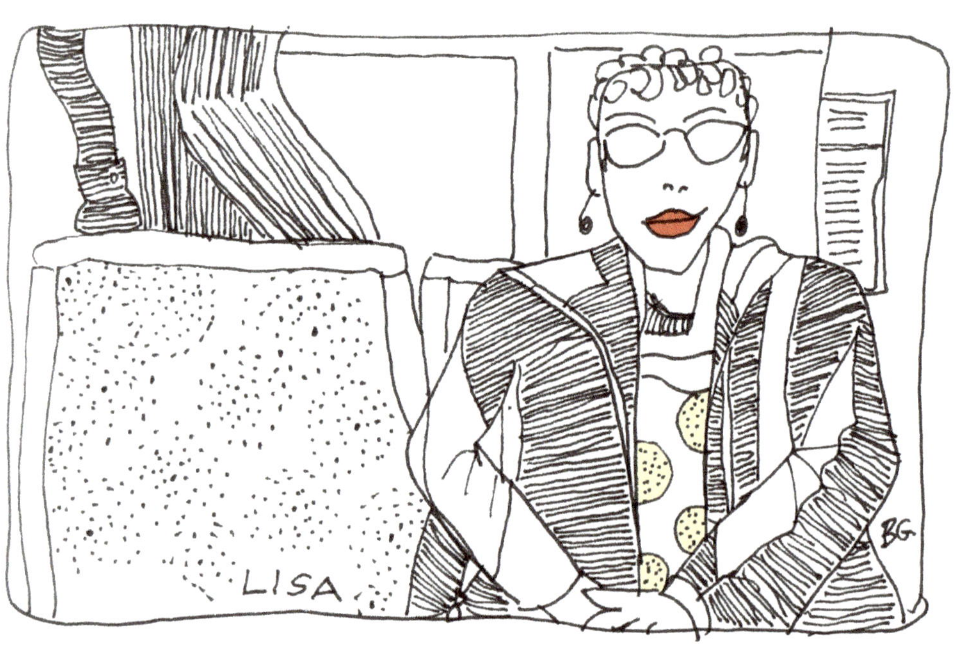
LISA
BG.

DID YOU KNOW?

Our light rail system has world-leading sustainability innovations. There is drainage throughout the track slab. This minimises rainfall run-off, protecting our local waterways and lakes.

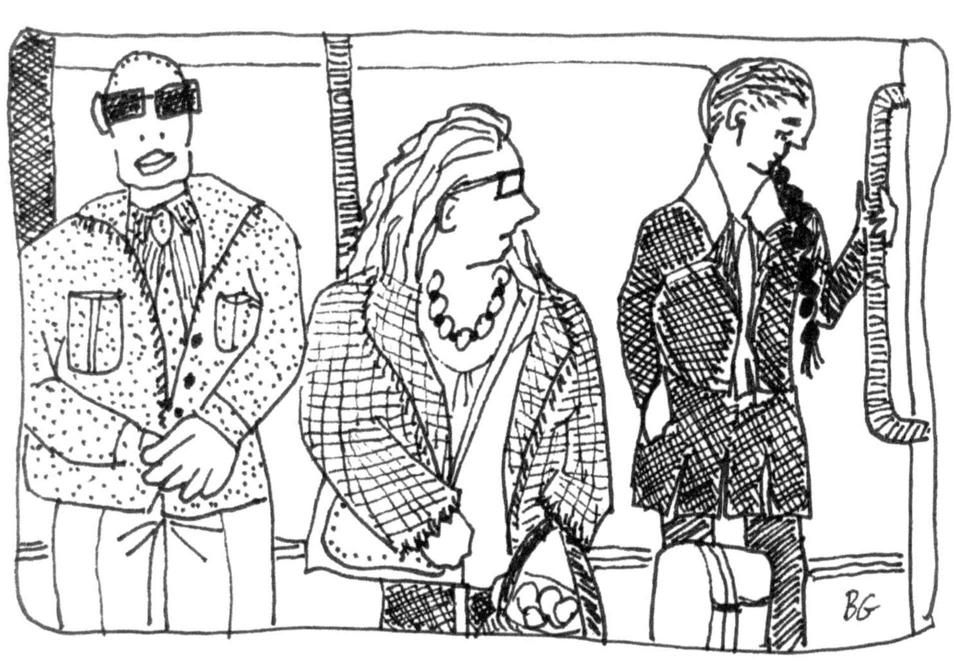
BG

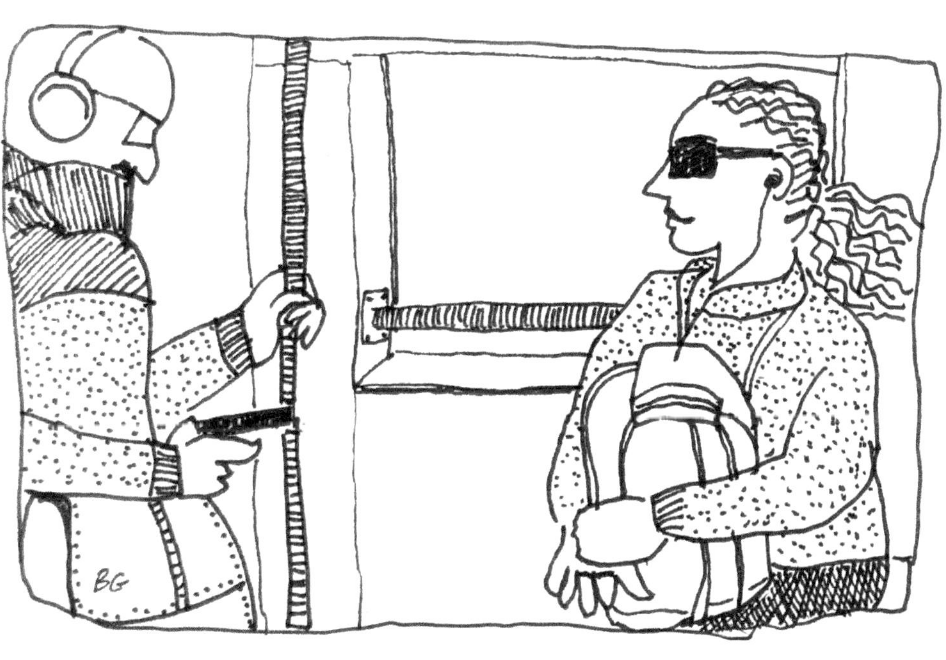

DID YOU KNOW?

During off-peak times (9.00 am to 4.00 pm weekdays), six Light Rail Vehicles operate with a 10-minute headway.

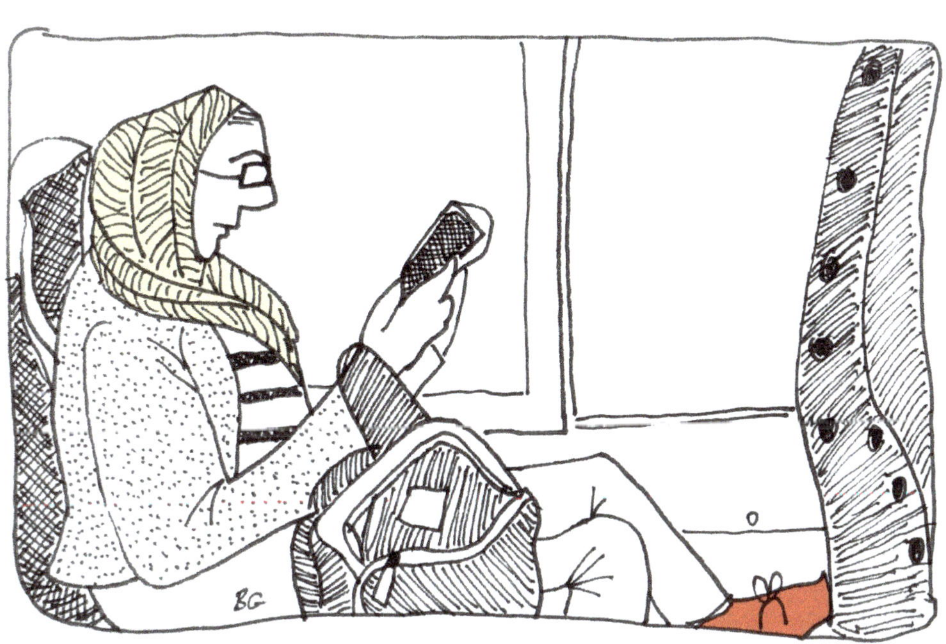
BG

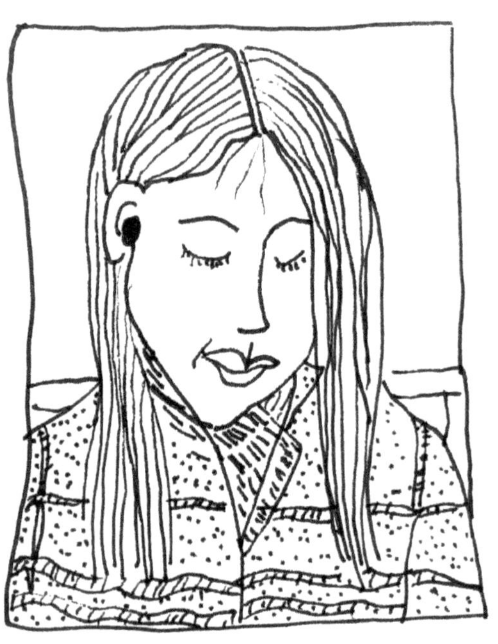

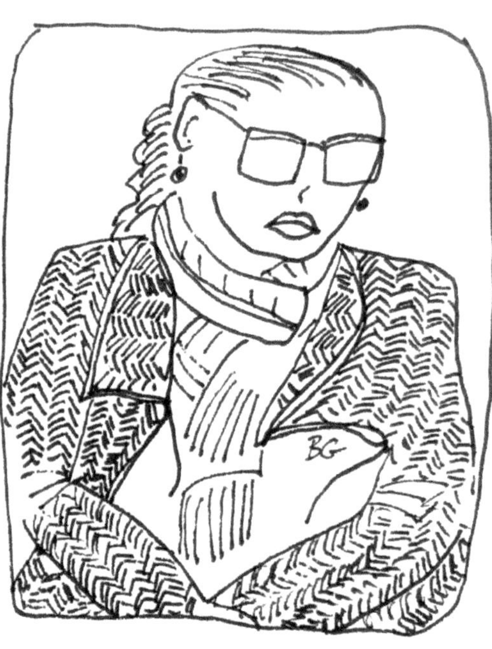
BG

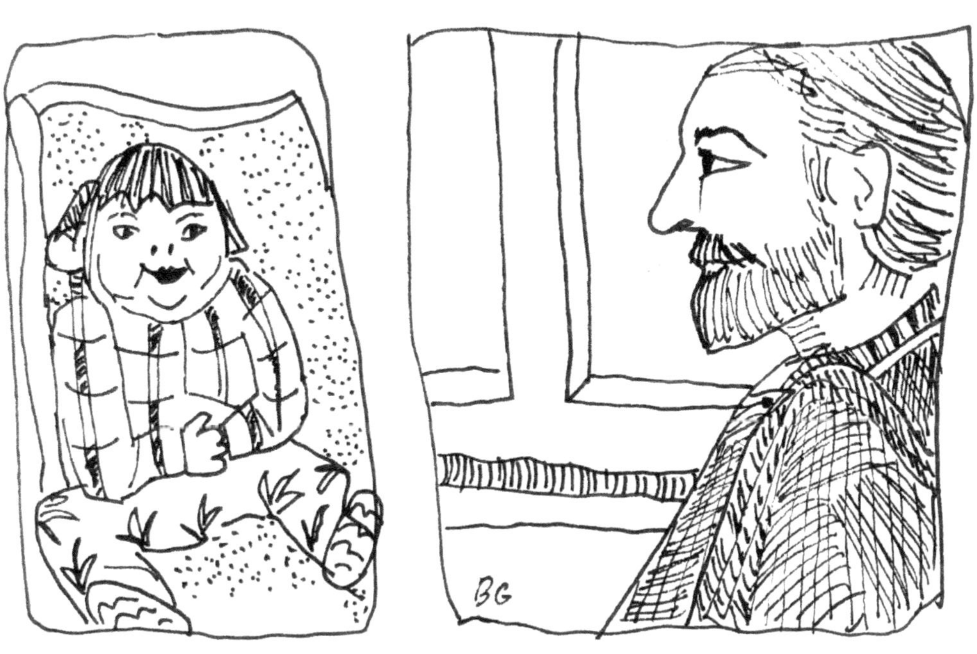

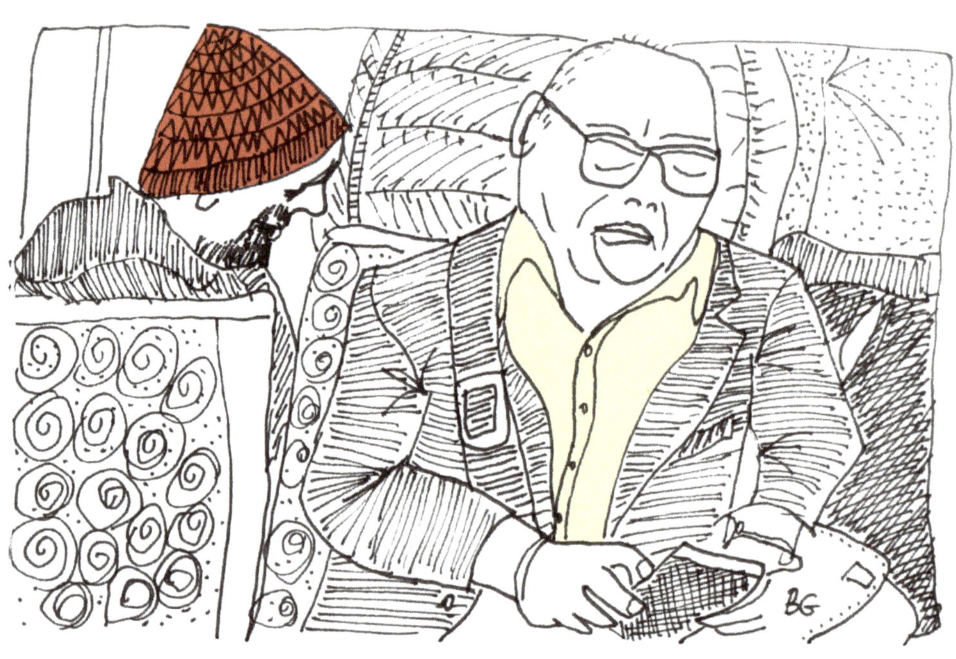

DID YOU NOW?

At peak times, 10 Light Rail Vehicles operate with a six-minute headway.

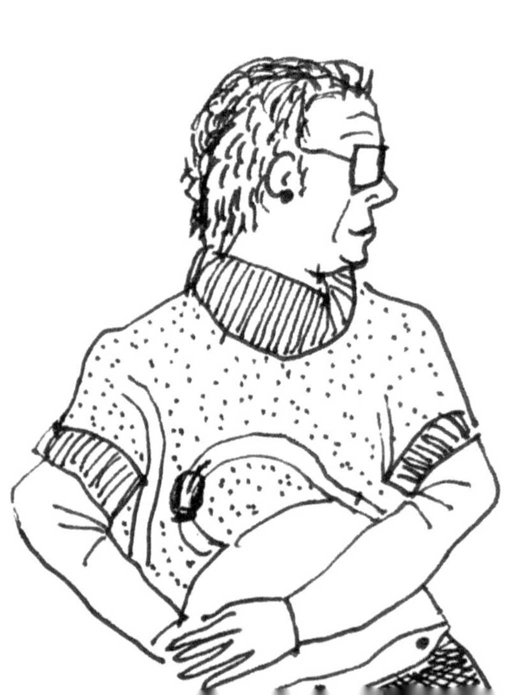

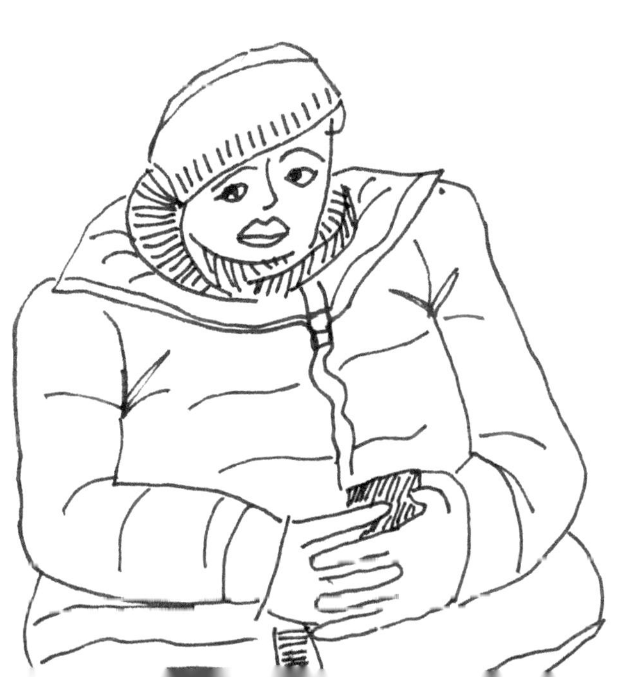

DO YOU KNOW THE NAMES OF ALL THE STOPS?

Gungahlin Place
Manning Clark North
Mapleton Avenue
Nullarbor Avenue
Well Station Drive
EPIC and Racecourse
Phillip Avenue
Swinden Street
Dickson Interchange
Macarthur Avenue
Ipima Street
Elouera Street
Alinga Street, City

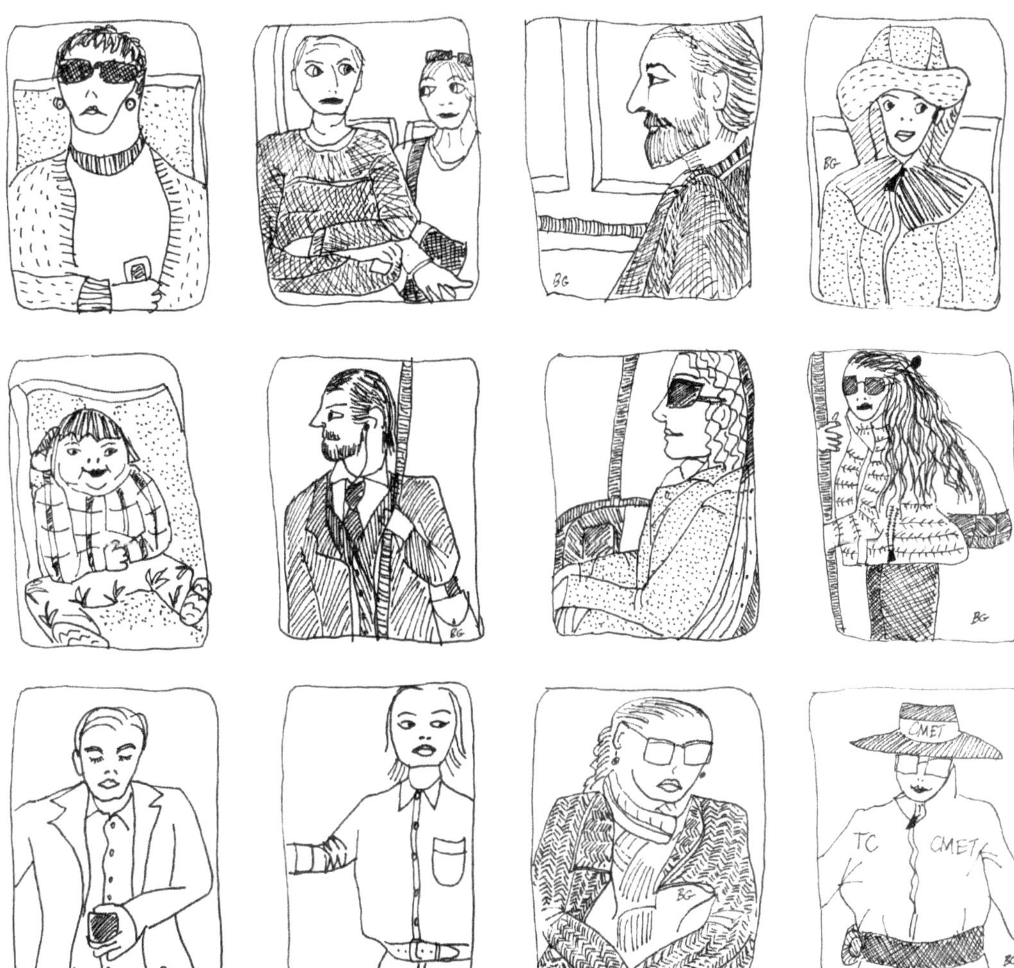
CMET
TC
CMET

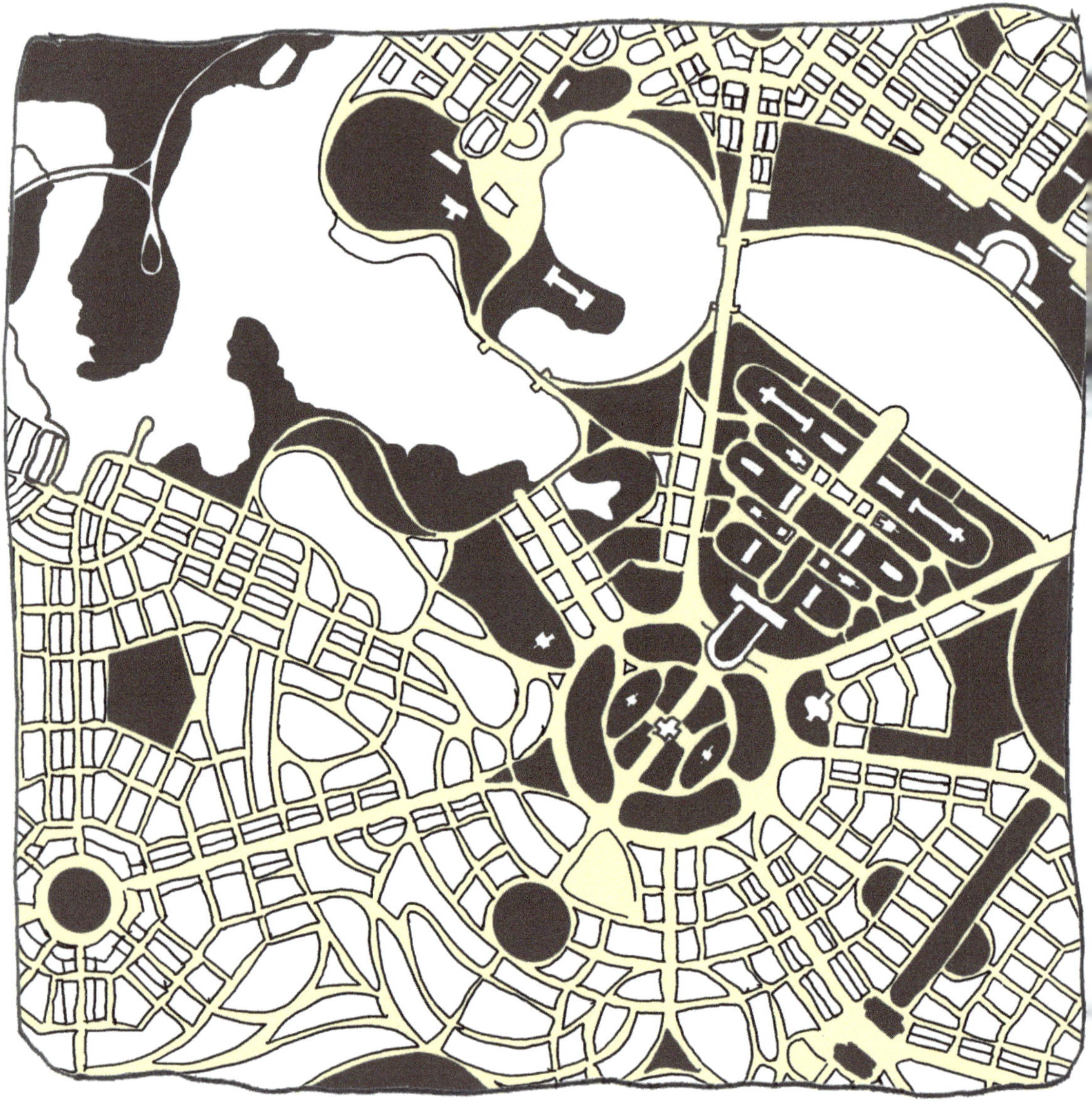

CANBERRA METRO

Light rail was already considered in the Walter Burley Griffin's early plans for the city. Most of arterial roads leading towards the city centre made provision for a wide corridor between the lanes in order to accommodate a future railway.

Keeping the light rail and cars separate makes Canberra Metro a fast and highly reliable mode of transport – unlike a typical tram system that has to share road space and is subject to traffic jams during peak hours.

The outstanding and iconic design of both the trains and the stations helps to make it easy for all travellers to appreciate and understand the network set-up.

Stage 1 currently terminates at Alinga Station in Civic, but plans exist to extend the line south to Woden.

MORE FROM THIS AUTHOR

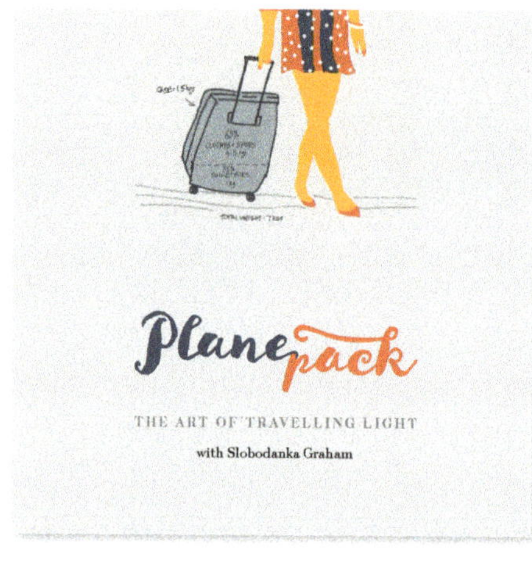

I fly and travel with carry-on luggage only. That's 7kgs. And yes, you can do it too!

At Planepack, discover the art of light travel: skip the queues; hop in and out of trains, boats and planes. Lose your addiction to heavy cases and you too will be a liberated light traveller.

I write, review, and illustrate light travel essentials, packing guides, travel tips - and how to travel with style and ease.

I hope *Planepack: the art of travelling light* inspires you to travel light.

www.planepack.com.au

Explore the National Library of Australia's secret spaces. See the stacks through the eyes of a sketcher.

For a brief period in early 2019, the author sat in Library corridors and sketched little known artefacts and objects. She captured reading room patrons and staff going about their Library business.

In *Hush: Secrets of the National Library*, Slobodanka has created an idiosyncratic sketch book that's sure to entertain and inform anyone interested in knowing more about the National Library of Australia.

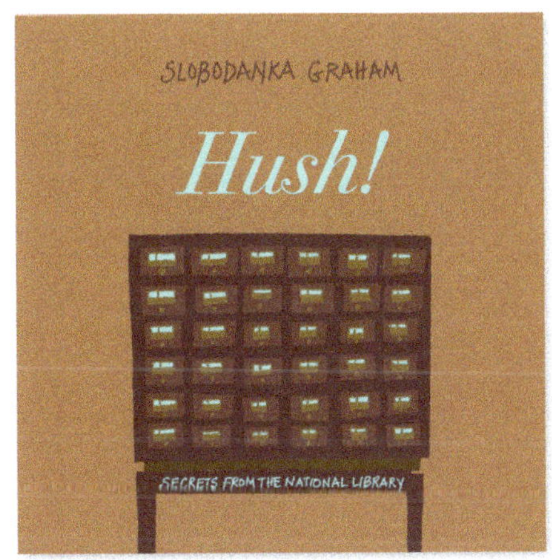

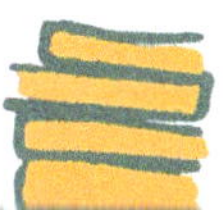

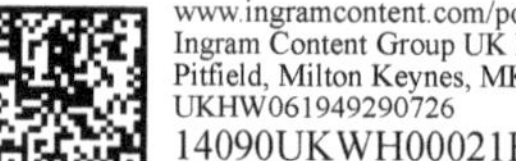
www.ingramcontent.com/pod-product-compliance
Ingram Content Group UK Ltd.
Pitfield, Milton Keynes, MK11 3LW, UK
UKHW061949290726
14090UKWH00021B/1145

9 780648 668633